The Quiet Whispers of Time

Meho Buljubasic

Order this book online at www.trafford.com
or email orders@trafford.com

Most Trafford titles are also available at major online book retailers.

Printed in the United States of America.

ISBN: 978-1-4669-1198-7 (sc)
ISBN: 978-1-4669-1197-0 (e)

Trafford rev. 01/17/2012

 www.trafford.com

North America & international
toll-free: 1 888 232 4444 (USA & Canada)
phone: 250 383 6864 ♦ fax: 812 355 4082

"To my family, friends, and Moirai"

The Time Cave

My eyes are closed with the frozen wave
it was my choice to become captive of the time cave
the world, the problems and the time itself
are captured in the book amongst many other on a dusty shelf

I am not sorry, for laying captive in the time cave
because I am finally set free of the powerful greed
of the silhouettes, illusions, and life that is lame
With the hope that it will not be the same

When sooner or later I open my blue eyes
I will see the world in the light arise
from the East and from the West
I will be new person that is just like the rest

San i sreca

Eh da sreca krila ima
Mogla bi doci letom svima
I usamljenom srcu sto vene
Na obronku litice snene
A mozda, rekoh mozda i do mene

Moj zivot je jedan lijepi san
I dok ga sanjam svaki dan
Sve ljepote ovoga mog svijeta
Smjestene su u dva prekrasna cvijeta

Bosna je cvijet lijepi sto krasi
Od ljepote sto ti oci mazi i pazi
Samo sta bjese onaj drugi cvijet
Nekad se cesto u snu zapitam i ja
Eh to je iskreno srce sto cistinom sija

Flake and the Snow

It is heavy yet it floats
In the air and in hopes
It's one of the many
That forms pure and white snow

It has no dreams
It has no particular hopes
It doesn't have a will
Its will is the wild wind

Never it questions its existence
Elevating far and far in the distance
Yet long path it needs to take
All to become both snow and the single flake

The Last Moment

The time has suddenly stopped
All hopes and wishes are now trapped
History, present and the future are now one
Twisted within the fate that is almost done

The time and the space are now wrapped
In a glamorous dance of an untainted light
There are no more ifs and buts
With the last breath and the last sight

Hey France Wake Up!!!

Have you seen the France?
In a ridiculous trance
While failing to glance
In a pure Bosnian dance

Hey France, wake up!!!
Why do you need a referee?
Or a whistle for a white spot blow
To save you from the Blue Bosnian call!

Bosna

Ne moze cudna Bosna
A da ne ostavi dojam
Kako kratko ime ima
A toliko sirok pojam

Za stranca je Bosna
Jedna rijec mala
toliko za njega mala
da je zaboravi iduceg dana

A za mene je Bosna sve
San i moja java
Moja prva ljubav
Koju i danas sanjam

Ne razumije neuk stranac
Sta to meni Bosna znaci
Niti koliko mi treba
dok sam sam ispod NJ neba

The Star of Somalia

How much does it cost?
To prevent Somalia's child to be lost
How is it to be the child of Somalia?
But to be hungry, poor, and lost.

We care how to make from our lives the most
While the star of Somalia is going to be lost!
Do we live in one planet under the same sky?
Or we live in different so we don't hear its cry

Is the tear of Somalia's star different than our?
Different in color, wealth, or maybe in power
Do we know this or we neglect the one?
That the same tear could be your or mine

Time and the Stranger

Time whispers the grey ode to the past
It has taken me sixteen summers to pass
To walk down this old street in my place
To let the Sun in the dawn tame my new face

I am now both the stranger in the new
I am the new in this very strange place
Only silhouettes of the past
Run in front of my new face

Is this the case of the aging?
Or this is another poetic drive?
I am not sure how to find the rest
For my alien soul captured between the East and the West

Layla and Majnun

It is 21st century and nice NJ noon
Yet I am roving like the blind Majnun
This love for us was a great cost
Now blind in the desert I am lost

One will ask whether it is worth
To lose the sight and yet move forth
One smile of Layla is dream yet not seen
Worth of being lost in love that is keen

All love twisted within chest
Will erupt in a great Moirai cast
I am not sure she hears these cries
I just want to see once more her eyes.

Love Between Rainbow and The Cloud

Something strange happened in the sky
A Cupido playing with his love bow
Aimed at the white cloud
And a colorful rainbow

Love has made cloud to fly fast
To reach the beautiful rainbow
To find his love fast
To build their love a beautiful nest

Yet rainbow is stubborn as usual
To more the cloud draws near
Its colors are beautiful and in instance
The rainbow runs further in the distance

Epic Dawn

In this beautiful epic dawn
Covered with the dew and the haze
I am thinking about our love
and its next beautiful phase

The day that we will seal
Our love into the eternity
In the moments of passion yet to feel
Together we will gaze upon a destiny

Very Sad Day

Today something went wrong
Once great love that was strong
Turned to a blast of colorful lies
While my ruptured heart silently cries

It's sunny outside, the Sun smiles
I don't believe it
I think it's dark
And the Sun lies

No the shine of Sun
Nor the smell of rose
Can replace the lost thing
Can revoke the last spring

I walked down the way
Towards the town that is now grey
I think about things I should do or say
I think about her every night and every day

Yet I find my verses lame
They are sad and they are same
Now Moirai while I speak in this pain
Know that my Sun will never rise up again

Today something went wrong
It's my heart that quietly cries
It has lost its beautiful lord
And verily every hope in this world

The Sun and the Moon

In this destiny where we hide and run
We have fallen in love so soon
My lovely as a shiny Sun
And me as a lonely Moon

Sun that burns and glows
Giving the light and a life to the Moon
The Moon that's trying to hide
In his mysterious dark side

She accepted the Moon and his hide
His temper and his dark side
Yet the Sun wants one more thing
To make Moon smile every night and morning

Sweet Reverie

Kiss or sweet death
And our love is yet taking a path
Ready I am for the future not yet seen
On this beautiful destiny's scene

Love that is crafted in a heat
In your love I want to fell so deep
Never want to leave that place
All I need is to keep looking at your face

The Storm and The Sun

My lips are sealed
But not my eyes
So that's where it stays
In this fall's love case

It's cold outside
But strangely I feel it is warm
Maybe it is a love
Or maybe a storm

Storm that rushes
Through my blood
And my mind
And the love that makes me fly

After the storm, we hope to see the Sun
Let that Sun shines then
Above us
If it has enough light, if it can

Where

Where can I be gone?
After these beautiful days
To follow up the Sun
Or to simply fade away

Where are why's and if's now?
Where is the dream?
Where is her love?
Does she hear my scream?

Oh Divine, and Almighty One
Please help us, to make it be
Please don't let this love to die
Please don't let her another cry

Let all curse, and pain go on me
Let all universe collide in me
Let the torment twist in my being
Let her be in her best reveries

I have one more wish before I go,
I want her to see
I want her to feel
She's all universe to me

Cold and dark NJ Night

Very cold and dark night
Yet colder it's within my heart
My love, that's my life so to say
Took the path, to go away

To go away from me
Take my future
With herself
And my reveries

Yet my love doesn't see
There is the river and the sea
River that brings us together when there is a love
Sea as for the two drops to become one

Neither the river, neither the sea
can now see, and more difficult to feel
What happen, what have I done?
Why my love does want to be gone?

All the questions, silence remains
Sea and the river fading away
I love her, love her, and love her
More than I ever had

My love, and my life
What I will ask you one more time
For the time yet to come, yet we need to take
Open your heart for our future's sake

White Dove and the World

She said she wants to give me the world
But she hopes at least her heart is enough
Oh my darling, you will happily feel and see
That your heart is a universe to me

You heart is a pure well
Where my universe dwells
You are the light reaching the empty scope
Giving my life very big hope

World is small, world is sometimes dark
Yet your light carries one single mark
While it upraises from the earth to above
It's carrying love, and hope like a white dove

The Time

The old watch is lazy
While letting the moments pass
Thus, those years are crazy
For passing so ridiculously fast

Every year is like the previous one
Let time pass fast and be done
But the precious moments near love
Make me feel young now

Ah! For a moment I thought
But maybe it was a dream
That the time had stopped
And that finally I am free

Tick! Tack! Says the old watch to me
It's time for you to awake
From that illusion and the reverie
Time never stops; it flows and it is not fake

The old watch covered with the dust
Has been witness of many events in the past
Yet long it counted the time with its face
While being long on my grandpa's old showcase

Sweet Violet (Fioletowy)

In this love one is sure
Many questions many truths
Seek for love seek for answers
Followed by the mist and shadow of the ancient

My love that my world stands upon
Sometimes draw near sometimes far
Until she understands after the strife
She is the Sweet Violet in the spring of my life

The Blue Rose

I stared at the lonely Moon
While it tamed the roses
The blue roses of my garden
Cowered with the fresh dew

Yet the most beautiful rose
Is not the one in my garden?
The most beautiful rose is the one
That is covered with the dew of my love.

The day she said yes

I was thirsty for a long time
Longer than one remembers
Looking to the pure well in every corner
For drop or two to tame the torment

I never lost the hope
Yet I lost my dream
That there is a pure well
Well of love and eternity

When sight was fading away
Slowly, slowly, and slowly
In my mind I heard her call
The rose in my hand was about to fall

I was on my knees
The rose in my hand
Haunted by the dire reveries
And getting power enough to stand

Her eyes, her jewels
Ignited the corner of my heart never was tamed
It starts giving me power giving me physics
To rise once more from the ashes like a forgotten phoenix

Then I spread my wings
I spread them wide
I had no fear
Nor I did hide

I jumped of the cliff
Jumped down high
Her voice reached me
Teaching me where to fly

I've risen to the skies
Some can say even higher
I was going towards the Sun
I spread my wings to dive in fire

Then, I saw her eyes
Blue aura around her
Everything was blue around
Her eyes, skies, air and the ground

We didn't speak
Nor let the word sneak of the lips
She spread her wings and jump high in atmosphere
And there we are phoenix and blue sapphire
What happened later is a mystery
Yet to come yet to be
I will not try to guess
I just wanted whole world to know she said
Yes, Yes, Yes,

Girl Without Heart

It was my destiny to find the space
In a place where love is cold and hard
To fell in love with the blue girl
Girl that doesn't have a heart.
She said she doesn't like the game
Nor the lovely truth that is fake
She doesn't like the fickle player
Nor the poems I write for her
This lovely being has its weakness
She plays hard yet she's witness
That love that comes with this drive
Is not another date or fake love
Nevertheless, she will do the same
To forget, ignore and run away
But there is mystery occupying her mind
Whether our hearts beat at the same time

The Fallen

With anxiety I entered the darkness
The corridors of pain, and relief of desire
Walking through the tunnels of love
Through mysterious whirlpool of time

My wings are broken, feathers are wet
I fell on my knees waiting destiny to met
I stand up and crawl towards the light
I saw your beautiful face in my sight

Dream

I wish to go to the highlands
With you
Close to the trees
Close to the place where mist sleeps

To lay down on the grass
And having you laying by me
And just talk with you
Talk till the night . . .

Talk until the Moon rises high above the sky
and the night covers us with the dreams
Moonlight on your face
In dreams you and me

Hand by hand walking in the dreams
Going to the far most places
To the distant galaxies
Places where Universe ends

Yet that is not enough for our love
We will, must go beyond
To the places where universe ends
Places no one yet transgressed

In the morning when I wake up
I will see sunshine taming your face
Those beautiful blue eyes will open up
And world will get one great love and a smile.

The End

It's time to make an end
To this poetic drive
To the few rhymes
To the precious lost time

I've turned to be player
Player of fate, player of hate
I've become a deserter
In a battle for future
I battle in hades

Disappearing

On this unusual day my heart is quite
Sometimes whispers word of two
Then stops, and become tired
Tired of past, tired of desire

My heart is not a rebellion
It doesn't beat to hurt
It doesn't beat to make others cry
It just needs a hope to hug

My heart is quite now,
Quite it will stay long
Distanced from the love
Distanced from the passion

It burns now unaccompanied
It is about for its final cast
To stop searching for affection
Quietly disappearing in the past
The end of game

The Golden Leaves

Golden leaves take their final flight
From the great heights to the dirty mud
Once they were green, they were high
Now they go down to become a crud

They remember the song of the wind
Spring and trembling under the sun
Now they go down, down and down
Down to the cold and black ground

They are not sorry for the Spring
Nor they feel sad for their life
They are sad to see tree bare
While hopelessly going to the ground

Two Souls

Every soul in a world and the heaven has its pair
Sometimes close sometimes far far away
Lonely Hearts that stay in the dusk, and stay in the far
Wait for a light of a destiny to break that dark

Once the destiny casts light on those two
They merge into one, merge from the two
And as a river that flows towards the distant sea
They bring they love to the eternity.

Town

Here I am standing above the local town
Standing on the crossroads of my life
Standing on the throne of the time
Staring at the town covered by the night

What a beautiful sight it is to be seen
Many ideas, dreams and loves
Rise above the town and glow
Followed by my wishes and the first snow

Two Angels whispering in the dark

Hey! You two whispering in the dark
Don't use my word as an infernos spark
To spark a fire, to spark a dislike
Ending our friendship, ending my time

Don't judge me, don't accuse me
Please don't ask me why?
Why my word has a truth
Yet it looks it contains a lie

The poems I write
Poems you judge
Are a flask of emotions
Hidden in my heart

I don't rule them
Because I don't know how
How do I write them?
Nor the place in my heart they hide

My two angels whispering in the dark
You can go to the place and give them a light
To take them out of darkness
To let them shine, and be my life.

Sunset

Please say Hi, my dear Sun
When you perish from the sky
Taking all the light, all the warmth
To the darkness, to the other side

You'll leave me in darkness
You'll leave me in bleakness
But please don't take my hope away
My dear Sun, I need hope to hideaway.

Young man and the sea

Once a young man sailed to the distant seas
To the promises to his desired dreams
He believed in good wind and hope
He was fearless, he was tough

When wind brought him to the land
He started to realize, he started to awake
Finally understanding the one
His wish was the place from which he has gone.

Alone

When all parties are gone
Together with the smiles, laughs
Maybe love and hate depart from my home
Behind the gate I stay very alone

Loneliness is the strange feeling
It can make you hard
It can make you strong
But it stands upon you like the curse

It follows you, it haunts you
It makes you strange, makes you feel alone
Whether you are behind the gate
Or in a million-souls living town

Where is my flock, where does it fly now?
Why have I departed, why do I cry?
Was it me to choose this doom?
To stay alone with the loneliness in this cold room.

Silent day in the Fall

It's silent rainy day in the Fall
Drop by drop, from the grey sky
Reminiscence and melancholy making a call
In the grey sky, and in the grey Fall.

It's now pain as a shadow of the bygone
Of verily nice moments, once in the past
Making us blue, remorseful, silent and shade
Not letting us be happy in this lovely Fall day

Surfing on the wave of time

I am surfing fast and high
High on the big waves of time
They will take me higher and higher
Higher than any of my previous desires . . .

Yet, I am waiting for big wave to come
To let me go higher, to let me fly
Fly from the seas to the high skies
To meet my call, passion, and love/Moirai

Life and Death

Every soul has its call
For the life and the death
And the destiny bestowed
On our life, and our hopes

Yet some of us struggle to see
Soon or later everything will cease
What is left of our blissful lives?
Moment or two looking towards the skies.

Talking

Is it talking the game of the tongue?
To force us eccentrically just to say
Without asking for the price
Soon or later we will have to pay

Well every word has its weight
Has beginning and the end
Emotion or feeling bearing with itself
Sometimes even love that one to other we send

But those of love are strong so much
That we shouldn't use sarcasm too much
Hence, they are both light and hard
They can pierce our mind, and verily our heart.

Feelings

We both got caught in a dream
In a sweet illusion, or maybe
In a dark and high reverie

There was no place to run away,
It was either to surrender,
or let the love fade away

Feelings that approached us
From every side, and every way
Are now only hostages of the trance
that simply faded away

Some Strange Feeling

You asked me did I like you
While destiny flew around in the air
Waiting to be hooked by the lover
And his blue clamorous plea

You are carved deep in my heart
My mind and my veins
Do you still need an answer?
You beautiful angel with a beautiful hair

Farewell

When I saw you
i have let one thought to run
from the deepest corner of my heart
it flew away to different time
and different space

so maybe
I said maybe
it's better if I am ambiguous

Hence I saw you happy
in a cast of light caught
in one single moment in the past

beautiful, happy and smiling
let it stay that way,
let me be confusing
let me go away

The Black Crows

The Black crows fly high
High above my ship and me
High into the skies
Waiting patiently for someone to die

Is it my turn, or it is my foe's
The Black crows don't ask, they are wise
They wait for the moment of weakness
Wait for the moment of demise

Don't look into the future
While staring into the dark past
Dark like the crow's wing
Elusive enough for crows to triumphal sing

Instead rise your head, to the blue skies
Feel the winds pushing your sails
Feel the time bringing the changes
Feel the raise of your pride again

Neither the black crows, nor their devious sound
Can harm you or your ship once again,
While it is the imprudent crows not to see
The victory coming towards us on this very shadowy sea

Birds and the Sun

When the Sun rises on the horizon
The few birds asked it why
Why the beams of light touch their wings
Or why do birds have to sing.

The only thing they know
It is not the choice, but it is a must
To sing the beautiful song of life
Like their ancestors did in the past.

Amerika

U ovoj zemlji satkanoj od snova
U more stapa se nada neka nova
Nada sto polako nestaje i lapi
Kao brza rijeka satkana od kapi

Nemirno je more u tamnoj noci
Dok ovaj osjecaj tuđine nece proci
Dok val vremena iz sna me budi
Kasno je postao sam neko drugi

Stecak

Budi se kamenu stari
Budi se trebas nama sada
Budi se dok krv vrije
Budi se dok iz rana krv lije
Budi se vodi nas sada
Budi se spasi nas sada
San ti treba to i znamo
Ali vrijeme dode tako
Da bez tebe nije lako
Budi se dok nije kasno

Automn

Automn is outside
Automn is in your heart
Leaves fall of the tree
Like the hopes in your heart

Maybe tired you are
My little rising sun
But there is mistery of tomorow
Coming together with the dawn.

Mojoj sudbini

Putujem po moru plavom
K'o Odisej u stara vremena
Srce mi zudi za ljubavi pravom
I za onom sto me iz daljine gleda

Zatrepti usamljeno srce moje
U visine misticne se digni
Idi do jedine ljubavi moje
I polako do sudbine stigni

Eh Reci mi oko moje plavo
Dok u dubine ovoga mora gledas
Zelis li da sudbinu dijelimo
I da budem ljubav koju trebas

Srebrenica

Sesnaest ljeta prodje
A on jos ne dodje
Mozda poneka silueta
U mojim mislima seta

Navrati me i podsjeti
Dadne mi nadu i cezne
Da je ziv i da ce doci
Dok sesnaesto ljeto vec ce proci

O oblaci u visinama skrivenim
Svjedoci ste bili tog sejtanskog zla
Recite mi dok majcinskim glasom vas molim
Da li je vasa kisa njegovu krv sprala

Koliko li ce jos ljeta proci
A moje dijete opet nece doci
I dok dusa tuzna bitku bije
Znam da je sehid i da mrtav nije.

Bosnjak

U neizvjesnoj sadasnjici
U buri vrtle povijesti
U buducnost hrli Bosnjak
Ponosno i bez straha
Dok ga prati val visoki
Sa bistrim kapima istine
Bosnjak se osvrne i osmjehne
Jer nema zlobe da je krije

Dijete Kabula

I dok kuca na vrata Kabula
Dugoocekivani Gost Ramazan
Kroz porusene i kaljave sokake
Kroci nevino dijete Kabula

Golo, gladno bosonogo i tuzno
Nailazi na ratnika jaka dva
Stid prekriva plastom ponosa
Nejako dijete, heroj Kabula

Printed in the United States
By Bookmasters